The Simplicity of Cultivating
Intimacy with God

K.I.S.S.

Keep It Simple, Saint

Edited by Ted Hillberg

K.I.S.S.

Keep It Simple, Saint

THE SIMPLICITY OF CULTIVATING INTIMACY WITH GOD

Kiss the Son, lest you die.
cf. Psalms 2:12

Edited by Ted Hillberg

Published by

G

Great Legacy Books
www.greatlegacybooks.com

G

Great Legacy Books
www.greatlegacybooks.com

For additional information contact:
Rachel M. Rasmussen
rachel@greatlegacybooks.com

Cover art: "Eternal Wave"
Copyright © 2018 by Bryan Hillberg.

Interior images (sketches of house, key, paper airplane, bread, and
hammer)
Copyright © 2018 by Bryan Hillberg.

ISBN: 978-0-692-10448-4

First edition

10 9 8 7 6 5 4 3 2 1

A note to the reader:

My dearest husband, Ted, lost his battle with cancer before this book went to print. I've never known another like my Ted—a man of deep conviction, love, loyalty, faith, vision and wisdom. These attributes were cultivated through much pain, struggle, and perseverance, especially in his early years. I guess the two best words I could use to describe him would be *worshipper* and *overcomer*. He touched so many of our lives, and for the better.

The following is the eulogy that Ted wrote for his grandmother's funeral many years ago. I came across it after he went home to the Lord. It was just *there*—folded up in a very random box of papers. Tears flowed as I read it, as it is a testament to the power of love in the generations and what we pour into them. Every summer, Ted and his siblings went to stay with his grandparents in Los Gatos, CA. Their influence on Ted was priceless, especially his dear grandma Mary. He wrote the following about her, and it so very much describes Ted as well:

> *Grandma was consistent, kind and giving, always right, bore no grudges. Did not carry forward any bitterness of past hurts or disappointments. She knew how to hand off blessing and 'bury the hatchet' of wrongs suffered. She knew that humor*

could plant 'hard truths' and laughter could cover 'minor indiscretions'. There was a vision in her to connect the foundations of family, history, and truth to the next generation who would be taking up the baton, to begin their leg of this journey. She did it with love, humor, humility, mercy, and grace.

May the seeds of life that she sowed in each of us, be watered with the gentle rain of His Spirit, to grow, to bless, and flourish in and for the next generation.

May the seeds of life that Ted sowed in each of us be watered with the gentle rain of His Spirit to grow, to bless, and to flourish in and for the next generation.

Always and Forever,
Debi Hillberg

DEDICATION

Written by Ted Hillberg

This collection is dedicated to the group of fifty or so men and women who have been getting together with me for the past four years or more, desperately seeking for God to move in power in our lives. We meet (as do thousands of others) because we are desperate: desperate to have God change us. We know we cannot live another day in our own strength and wisdom. And, we are desperate to have Him, who is able to strip away all flesh and blemish from His Bride, so that all our reflection of His love is refined to its most simple and pure expression... nothing more, and nothing less.

As I was reminded by my friend, Joseph Appler, the Apostle Paul himself feared that the knowledge and experience of believers in Christ could become so "complex" as to dilute our pure and simple devotion to our Savior.

---

*But I am frightened, fearing that in some way you will be led away from your **pure and simple devotion** to our Lord, just as Eve was deceived by Satan in the Garden of Eden.*

2 Corinthians 11:3 (TLB, emphasis added)

*But I am afraid that, as the serpent deceived Eve by his craftiness, your minds will be led astray from the **simplicity and purity of devotion** to Christ.*

2 Corinthians 11:3 (NAS, emphasis added)

TABLE OF CONTENTS

PREFACE

Ted Hillberg

Kiss the Son, lest you die. (cf. Psalms 2:12)

The title of this book was chosen for two reasons. The first reason lies in what the acronym "KISS" represents. The acronym stands for "Keep It Simple, Stupid!" It came from the U.S. Navy in 1960. The K.I.S.S. principle states that "Most systems work best if they are kept simple rather than complicated; therefore, simplicity should be the key goal in design and unnecessary complexity should be avoided." For the purpose of this book, we'll render the meaning to "Keep It Simple, Saint!" The second reason is in the symbolism of the kiss in Psalms 2:12: in order to live, we simply have to kiss the Son of God. Simply kiss the Redeemer. The title "KISS" captures the essence of living a life of intimacy with God.

This book will explore what it practically looks like to "kiss the Son" in the critical areas of our personal walk with the Redeemer of all mankind.

Events from the past five years highlighted for me the complexity that had crept into every corner of my life. This complexity had almost completely strangled my ability to express my love for my Savior. As I was constantly running to maintain my routines, relationships, work, finances, and ministry, I longed to stop and simply kiss my Lord. However, the felt need to keep running was difficult to resist. These complexities in my daily life barricaded me from what I desired most: a pure and simple relationship with Jesus.

I began to see that I was not alone in my frustrations. Many of my friends, both saved and un-saved, were bound up in the same struggle concerning the complexities of life.

It was around this time that I was reminded, by God and by other believers, of the simplicity of the life God has called us to. The yoke of the Spirit is easy, and the burden of the Lord is light. Yet in my life, the yoke of spiritual life was very hard, and the burden of walking as a child of the King was very heavy. I yearned for release from the weight. I wanted freedom from the chains of complexity. I sought my Father for how to change my reality to match His promises. He reminded me of truths I had seen walked out before me in the lives of other believers I knew. In addition, He strengthened those relationships in my life that clarified for me the simple ways I could walk out His call and commission daily.

There are five critical disciplines that God calls us believers to actively participate in. Through these disciplines, we express our giftings, love, testimony, and all else that is a holy reflection of our gratitude and adoration for our Lord. It is in the simplest expression of these disciplines that we find the most righteousness and purity. Our righteous, pure expressions become a "sweet smelling aroma" to the Lord. They alone remain as gold, silver, and precious stones in the house we are building upon His foundation. Only they endure the fire of testing.

The five critical disciplines of the life of intimacy with God are these: faith, worship, love, expression, and ministry. We will study these five disciplines in depth throughout this book. I have been blessed with strong relationships with several dynamic men and women of God over the years, four of whom I've asked to join me in writing this book. Together, we will go deep in exploring the practical aspects of our spiritual walk. We will expand our understanding of how God would have us be "pure, simple" reflections of Himself. Together, we will learn to grow into the most beautiful Bride of Christ—perfect, spotless, and without blemish.

My prayer is that as you read these pages, you will see fresh facets of who God is through the eyes of these saints. I pray that you will glean from the wisdom they have collected over a lifetime of constantly growing in God. As you read from the overflow of their hearts, I pray that you will be as blessed by them as I have been over the years. They are constant testimonies of His grace—servants delivering His mercy and healing.

As you will discover through this book, the key to cultivating an intimate relationship with God is pure and simple devotion to Him. Get ready to strip your life down to the simple things. Simply kiss the Son to become fully alive.

CHAPTER ONE

Simple Worship

Caleb Quaye

KEEP – To Retain and Hold on to

Let the word of Christ dwell in you richly in all wisdom; teaching and admonishing one another in psalms and hymns and spiritual songs, singing with grace in your hearts to the Lord. And whatsoever ye do in word or deed, do all in the name of the Lord Jesus, giving thanks to God and the Father by [H]im.

Colossians 3:16-17 (KJV)

The attitude of worship is one of the simplest, yet deeply profound, things in which a person can be involved. It is a wonder to think that we delight to participate in something that satisfies us at the deepest levels of our being, and yet, that in which we participate is not initiated by us. Instead, our worship is initiated by the One to whom we offer worship. This worship, then, is an act of faith, since it is directed toward the invisible One who gives us the power to worship. How amazing it is to ponder the fruit of His power in us: since the day we received His mercy, the rest of our lives are caught up in the ceaseless activity of offering worship, not only in songs and music, but in choices that result in words and deeds that honor the One whom we cannot see!

We love Him because He first loved us. Since the fall of Adam, God has pursued us, seeing us from afar as His bride-to-be and household-to-become. Furthermore, through Christ and His sufferings, God has purchased us at Calvary's cross. We have been sealed and filled by the Holy Spirit so that we are kept as the object of His affections. We are ever present before Him as His children and members of His household.

The Spirit himself bears witness with our spirit that we are children of God.

Romans 8:16 (ESV)

    Reflecting God's affections toward us, now that we have Christ in us by the gift of the Father through the Holy Spirit, *our* hearts are moved *toward Him* in worship so that we may possess the object of *our* affections, which is our Savior, Christ Jesus our Lord!

    By nature we are creatures of possession. We pursue relationships because we want to possess (or keep) the object(s) of our affections. We cannot possess Christ bodily, of course. But we *can* experience and possess His presence and the working of His Spirit.

Repent, then, and turn to God, so that your sins may be wiped out, that times of refreshing may come from the Lord

Acts 3:19 (NIV)

    Significantly, those who profess to believe in the Lord, but who are not active participants in worship, tend to live with a sense of distance from the Lord. By contrast, those who are worshippers are very aware of His presence. They are refreshed in Him.

Oh that men would praise the Lord for [H]is goodness, and for [H]is wonderful works to the children of men! And let them sacrifice the sacrifices of thanksgiving, and declare [H]is works with rejoicing.

Psalm 107:21-22 (KJV)

Worship that touches the heart of God keeps us in His presence. This worship begins with giving thanks. When we thank him for who he is, we see and feel that it is part of the nature of God to want to be present with us. As we recall on Christmas, one of the names of God is Emmanuel, meaning "God with us." When we worship the One who said He will never leave us nor forsake us, we experience the knowledge that He desires to *keep* us.

IT – The Word of God, and Faith in God

Worship is a means of restating and remembering God's truth for the purpose of life enrichment, effective witness, and kingdom fruitfulness. The Apostle Paul encourages the church to use psalms, hymns and spiritual songs to edify one another in the truth. In a similar way, parents teach nursery rhymes to help children forge truths in their minds. When we worship God, truths about God become central in our minds.

Truths from God are a catalyst for faith. Without them, we are unable to hear God or know Him. God's truth helps us with life enrichment, effective witness, and kingdom fruitfulness.

So then faith cometh by hearing, and hearing by the word of God.

Romans 10:17 (KJV)

Worship is vital to faithful living because worship refreshes our hearts in the presence of the Lord. This refreshment allows us to hear the word of the Lord, which in turn allows us to live our lives by faith. When we live by faith, we simply take the Lord at His word. This faith is the basis of life transformation, moving us "from glory to glory." In this way, worship develops our character, empowering us to advance the kingdom and overcome hell!

When we lead people in worship, we are leading them out of slavery. In Exodus 5:1, the first order of business from God was to have Moses bring the broken people of Israel, who had lost most of their identity, to a place of worship. God knows that people who labor under the slavery of abuse, low self-esteem, identity crisis, and hopelessness need most of all to stand in His presence and worship Him.

It is in His presence that we find out who we are and that we are loved greatly by the One who created us.

Know ye that the LORD [H]e is God: it is [H]e that hath made us, and not we ourselves; we are [H]is people, and the sheep of his pasture.

Psalm 100:3 (KJV)

In today's culture, our obsession with image and perfecting formulas drives us to complicate our *form* of worship. The New Testament definition of worship, however, is simple: **just show up**. Consider Paul's description of worship:

Therefore, I urge you, brothers and sisters, in view of God's mercy, to offer your bodies as a living sacrifice, holy and pleasing to God—this is your true and proper worship. Do not conform to the pattern of this world, but be transformed by the renewing of your mind. Then you will be able to test and approve what God's will is—[H]is good, pleasing and perfect will.

Romans 12:1-2 (NIV)

What I love about this verse is what I refer to as the "omission of condition". This simply means that whatever condition we are in, the cross of our Lord qualifies us to stand in His presence to worship Him and thereby be changed. Our disqualifications are omitted. The emphasis in this verse is to "offer your bodies," which means just *get there*, warts and all. He will take care of the rest, and He will separate us from the slavery of our times.

He sent [H]is word, and healed them, and delivered them from their destructions.

Psalm 107:20 9KJV)

Scripture reminds us of the transformative power of worship. More "surgery" goes on in worship than we know. Here are two examples of how worship transforms us:

1. *Worship provides hope in the face of nothing.* Isaiah 54:1 encourages us to start worshiping in times of barrenness. In the face of nothing, start singing.

2. *Worship breaks strongholds to make room for the truth to be preached.* In Acts 16:23-34, Paul and Silas were worshiping in the Philippian jail, and the account of what took place is as follows:

11

And suddenly there was a great earthquake, so that the foundations of the prison were shaken: and immediately all the doors were opened, and every one's bands were loosed.

Acts 16:26 (KJV)

Worship is the most powerful force for transforming us from the inside out.

SIMPLE – Saying "Thank You" with a Kiss

Jesus said that in order to enter the kingdom of heaven, one must have childlike faith (not childish). Childlike faith implies simplicity and purity of motives, thought, and actions. For this reason, I think it is the simplicity and purity of our worship that Jesus admires.

To illustrate childlike worship, imagine a young child who is learning to draw. All of their attention is focused on creating a picture they can't wait to present to their mom or dad. Some kids paint or scribble frantically because they are so excited at the prospect of giving something they have created as a gift to their parents. Others take a long time to complete the project because they want to make it as perfect as they can in order to please their parents. The simple yet profound motive behind both methods is *love*. The child will do anything they can with their newly

12

discovered creative gifts to express their love for their parents.

Just as a young child, we too can come before our Father in heaven in the form of artistic creativity, or of simply living life with God in mind, in order to express our love to Him. That love is deep within us, and it is a joy that longs for completion. The completion of this joy is simply to hear the Father saying, "That's great," "That's wonderful," "Thank you so much," "Can you do me another one?" or "Well done!" Someone once said that our worship is like drawings that our Father in heaven loves to stick on His refrigerator!

When we get to heaven, we hope to hear the Father's words to us, "Well done, good and faithful servant." These words mean that we have lived a life reflecting His character. This is only possible when worship is at the center of our lives.

The Greek word for worship, *proskuneo*, means to kiss, like a dog licking his master's hand! This kiss is a response of passion; it is not something that is analytically thought through. We kiss because we *love*—plain and simple. It is the same passion with which the child draws the painting.

In the complicated church culture of our times, there are never-ending debates over the form of worshipping God. We debate worship style, trends in worship, cultural relevance in worship, traditional versus contemporary, alternative and emerging church worship, loud or soft,

Boomer or Gen-X or Millennial worship, and so on. These debates go on in endless circles of fear and formula as people try to arrive at the perfect form that will satisfy all theological positions and institutional insecurities.

Then turning toward the woman [H]e said to Simon, "Do you see this woman? I entered your house; you gave me no water for my feet, but she has wet my feet with her tears and wiped them with her hair. You gave me no kiss, but from the time I came in she has not ceased to kiss my feet. You did not anoint my head with oil, but she has anointed my feet with ointment. Therefore I tell you, her sins, which are many, are forgiven—for she loved much. But he who is forgiven little, loves little." And [H]e said to her, "Your sins are forgiven."

Luke 7:44-48 (ESV)

Worship "in spirit and in truth" has nothing to do with style or formula. It does, however, have everything to do with love. It has to do with giving the most creative and passionate kiss that we can. We do this naturally when all of our faculties are focused on the Lamb of God who came to take away the sins of the world and deliver us from darkness. He brought us into His kingdom, and we are free to simply say "thank you" with a kiss.

SAINT – Worship and the Restoration of Sonship

The New Testament term "saint" refers to the character and identity of a believer. One of the incredible benefits of worship is the restoration of our identity as *sons of God*. Paul tells us:

Now therefore ye are no more strangers and foreigners, but fellowcitizens with the saints, and of the household of God.

Ephesians 2:19 (KJV)

Our identity in Christ is most probably the central battleground for believers in our times. The enemy loves to create confusion in this area. Yet, it is precisely in this area that worship gains the victory. It is in our times of worship that the Father loves to tell us once again who we are:

The Spirit himself bears witness with our spirit that we are children of God.

Romans 8:16 (ESV)

King David understood the value of sonship. In Psalm 2, he alludes to a difference between two types of people:

15

those *who make their plans apart from God* on the one hand, and those *whom God identifies as sons* on the other. He starts by saying, "Why do the nations rage and the people plot a vain thing?" Plans made apart from God, especially against God's anointed, are futile. The counsel of man sports *NO CONTEST* against the sovereignty of God! People in their broken nature, in their rage for control, with desire to be godlike, conspire against the Lord and His anointed; but God, in His sovereignty and abundant goodness, conspires for the benefit of those He calls sons.

How precious also are thy thoughts unto me, O God! how great is the sum of them! If I should count them, they are more in number than the sand.

Psalm 139:17-18a (KJV)

David continues in verse 4, "The One enthroned in heaven laughs." God has a sense of humor! He finds our vanity laughable. David reveals that the key to humility is found in *identity*. He says in verse 7, "I will proclaim the Lord's decree: He said to me, 'You are my son; today I have become your father.'"

David knew that he was God's son. He was secure in his identity. The knowledge of our identity as sons and daughters of God is a foundational piece of our worship. We come to God as sons, not as victims or accidents.

Our Heavenly Father's response to this humble attitude of sonship is always one of blessing. God replies to His son in verse 8: "Ask me, and I will make the nations your inheritance, the ends of the earth your possession." The counsel of the world focuses us on our condition in the world, which is invariably poor and negative, constantly fueling low self-esteem. The counsel of God, by contrast, constantly reminds us of our position in Him as members of the household of God, His sons and daughters.

David wraps up his Psalm with the advice, "Therefore, you kings, be wise." As New Testament believers, we understand it is wise to present ourselves to Jesus with the right attitude in worship. David continues with the strong motivation to follow his advice, "Kiss [H]is son, or [H]e will be angry and your way will lead to your destruction, for [H]is wrath can flare up in a moment. Blessed are all who take refuge in [H]im."

Worship is the means by which we declare our trust in the Lord. Therefore, as sons and daughters of God, may we never cease to present ourselves to Jesus in worship. May we come to Him with a kiss that seals our trust in Him. May we rejoice in the blessings of our Heavenly Father. May we delight in the call to be saints in His kingdom.

ABOUT THE AUTHOR
Caleb Quaye – Simple Worship

Written by Ted Hillberg

I have had the opportunity to develop a close relationship with Caleb that has grown over the past 30 years. Although everyone who reads this would be extremely impressed with his professional pedigree, that is not the reason I asked him to contribute to this book. Caleb's lineage is rooted in a native tribe of Ghana which, for centuries, has been appointed and anointed to function as worship leaders. The correlation to the tribe of Levi is not coincidental. Caleb has been uniquely gifted to bridge the gap between the spiritual act of worship and the physical expression of music genetically imbedded in our soul. The "interpreted worship" that comes from our spiritual hearts under his leadership is a pure, simple, itinerant expression of our simple adoration for our Savior. The very nature of Caleb's ministry calls us to a gut-level expression that cannot be clouded by any complex performance, or any other veil that the "flesh" would attempt to filter our worshipful expression through. When Caleb plays, sings, writes, or leads in worship, the hearer cannot help but "fall in step" in the progression to the throne, culminating in that pure expression of our hearts' cry—the sort of expression that we all come anticipating and yearning for when we come together as worshippers.

CHAPTER TWO

Simple Love

Henry Washington

Throughout Scripture the Lord calls us to love one another (Rom. 13:8), live in harmony (Rom. 12:6), and serve each other (Gal. 5:13). Simple love has many functions to make it work. Here are a few:

1. Obedience

2. Forgiveness

3. Vision

4. Humility

5. Courage to walk away

Obedience

The Christian life is, to put it simply, walking obediently with God (John 15:1-17). Obedience is by far a decision of the heart. Obedience is so important to God that Jesus made a point to model it His whole life on earth.

God has shown me in the Bible that He *perfects His love* in those who keep His commands (1 John 2:5). Our obedience is a sign by which we can know that we are in Him. When we are in Him, we experience genuine love. Once we experience genuine love, we can give it to others.

Genuine loves means loving people for who they are, not for what they have achieved in life. It means loving them without restriction. If you must be in control of what another person does in order to love them, then you do not understand what true love is all about.

Looking at the love of Jesus Christ at the cross, we see the most perfect demonstration of love to be found. Jesus was obedient even unto death. Love is what prompted God to send Jesus to save the world. Because of what God did by sending Jesus Christ to die for us, we now have a demonstration of love as the key to life. Our sight of this love determines the type of life we will live.

God began perfecting His love in *my* heart as I made myself obedient to His Word. He began to perfect His love in my heart so that I could rear two children in the nurture and admonition of the Lord Jesus Christ. There is something about rearing children that brings out more love in a person, along with the presence of God. In order for me to love two children (and others in my life), I had to release one of the areas of my life that God wanted me to release to him—and that was the area of "control".

Forgiveness

Jesus has shown me in my life that love has several enemies. One is *fear*; another is *hurt*. Sometimes we refuse to love because of these two enemies. From my past life, I developed the type of heart that refused to love people— including family. Even after I began walking with God, I still held love back. As I continued living in fear and hurt, I was unable to trust. My lack of love continued until the Holy Spirit spoke to my heart and said, "That is disobedience."

The Holy Spirit said that God's kind of love is directed outward towards others. Living in fear is not loving one another. God's kind of love goes against our natural inclinations. In fact, it is only possible for us to demonstrate it if God helps us set aside our own desires and instincts. With God's help, we can give love while expecting nothing in return. In this way, we become more Christ-like.

How do we learn to love this way? The Bible gives us the basis for understanding true love.

We have come to know and have believed the love which God has for us. God is love, and the one who abides in love abides in God, and God abides in him. By this, love is perfected with us, so that we may have confidence in the day of judgment; because as He is, so also are we in this world. There is no fear in love; but perfect love casts out fear, because fear involves punishment, and the one who fears is not perfected in love. We love, because He first loved us. If someone says, "I love God," and hates his brother, he is a liar; for the one who does not love his brother whom he has seen, cannot love God whom he has not seen. And this commandment we have from Him, that the one who loves God should love his brother also.

1 John 4:16-21 (NAS)

And so we know what the true love of God is. When we know it, we come to rely on it. But once we really know God's love, we can't help but reflect that love toward others.

Because of these words from the Father, and because of my obedience to them (which was a learning process), fear no longer has a place in my life. Instead, perfection of His love in my heart started a growth process that removed hurt. I gained eyes to see the love my children needed from me.

As my life progressed, the Lord continued to reveal that I must surrender the area of control. I had a compulsion to control situations in my life. That compulsion was born out of my fear of hurt. If I could exert control, then I could keep from being hurt by others. This was the area in which I could not walk in trust of the Lord.

Because of my refusal to surrender this area of control, the result was two-fold in the events of my life. First, it held back the answers to the prayers of my heart for almost 15 years. Second, it prevented God from working in me and others, specifically my ex-wife. It prevented God from being the Author and also the Finisher of the work of faith in us.

Yet, because of His great love, faithfulness, grace, and mercy, God continued to work in my heart (in spite of my years and years of rebellion). He worked His love and forgiveness in and through me. He brought about the change in His timing, in accordance with my eventual obedience. Obedience is in love, which unlocks forgiveness.

Vision

In my early years of marriage and family life, I thought that being an aerospace employee, making a lot of money, owning nice cars and a beautiful home, and gaining lots of friends were the greatest achievements possible. But I was wrong. Ecclesiastes provides us with an accurate picture of "emptiness" as we search outside the love of God for fulfillment. People around us still pursue the same empty goals. They look at wealth, pleasure, and success to get meaning in life.

A few years back, my daughter got married. Shortly after that, she announced that she and her husband were going to have a child—my first grandchild. It soon became apparent to me that the event of this child's birth was another part of God's plan to orchestrate an encounter with a new dimension of God's love. During this time, I witnessed acts of great love and forgiveness from family members as we got together to celebrate new life. This love inspired within each of us a new vision of God's goodness and grace.

Before these events, God had been "grooming" each of us individually in His presence, to teach us love, humility, and forgiveness. Now, as we gathered together to celebrate the birth of this grandchild, our individual visions joined together to produce a far greater vision of God's grace flowing through us to each other—and beyond. God used our joy as a catalyst to experience His kindness and to see the greatest treasures in our midst.

The Lord has revealed more to me about love through the Scriptures, especially, 1 Thessalonians 1:3. Here Paul writes about the "labor of love." After studying these particular verses, the Lord told me more about the forms of labor of love that we perform daily. Those labors help us become more like Jesus. The labors that He revealed to me are these:

1. Keeping His word.

2. Stamping out fear.

3. Working biblical truths into our lives.

4. Forgiving others.

5. Expanding our vision of God's goodness and grace.

As we labor toward perfection in these ways—perfection being "an exact meeting of the need"—the Lord perfects His love in us.

In I Corinthians 4:20, we read that the kingdom of God isn't a matter of talk, but of power. His "power" is *simple love*, the same love that He says "covers a multitude of sins."

During the period between the announcement of the impending birth of my granddaughter and the date of birth, the Lord moved in a very dramatic way in all of our lives (mine especially) concerning obedience in forgiveness. He continued to press on me, day and night, the truth that obedience to and in forgiveness would unlock the key to His love being manifested to someone He has loved since the day of her birth—my children's mother.

She had been brought up since her childhood in the "black Muslim" faith, which held her in bondage throughout her life. Through the years of frustration between us, and the years of her own battles, there was still a faithful call of God on her life, along with the promise of Romans 11:29— "The gifts and calling of the Lord, are irrevocable." The Lord began to work in me a vision for her that required my calling out for and declaring her forgiveness. He had moved me from cursing to healing, and ultimately to blessing who she is, and what He will and has done for her.

In our somewhat complex lives, we can easily lose our focus on the greatest of the attributes of the kingdom: love. For love is the "first" fruit of the Holy Spirit—not the second, third, or fourth, but the *first*. That is why God has given us the Holy Spirit: to empower us to a life of loving obedience. It is He (the Holy Spirit) who helps us labor in love. But we must also surrender to His work in us.

Humility

As the time for the birth drew near, the Lord began to burden me to take action on this newfound vision and transformation in our family. The Lord began to speak to me that I needed to humble myself, to obey the commandment to forgive, and to loose the chains of the enemy. The Lord spoke to me with specific instructions. He told me to call my ex-wife and talk with her about the vision of life for the new family that was being constructed. So, I did just that.

As I spoke with my ex-wife about the value and blessing of the child (and my daughter) having a loving and supportive relationship with her, she wholeheartedly agreed. The peace of the Lord began to fill the conversation. I confessed my anger and resentment for all the past history of our failed marriage and relationship. I expressed my repentance and sorrow for how I treated her, which I

28

acknowledged was a driving force in her rebellion against me. I told her that for me, and for us (the whole family), to move on in the Lord, I needed—and badly wanted—her to forgive me.

Her answer was an emphatic, "NO!" I was a little stunned; but she went on in her reply with, "I want to ask you to forgive me, from the bottom of your heart, for what I have done to you."

My response was a hearty, "Yes!" But she repeated the request again. Again, I told her I forgave her. Again, she repeated the request.

It was then that the Lord revealed to me that her repeated requests had nothing to do with her believing my response. She needed the assurance (in her spirit) that the man who for so many years had talked about Jesus would practice what he had preached so loudly. She was waiting for me to address her (and my) past from the stance of love, not from anger.

From this experience, I understand that we, as His children, are always under attack from the enemy in many areas of our lives. The enemy's attack is to cause us to harbor bad feelings against others so that we won't forgive them. He may even try to incite betrayal or fear. All of these feelings can hinder our labor of love and our reaching out to others in His name.

From childhood on, we are urged to show love to and for others. But the real test of our love for God is how we treat the people right in front of us—our family members and fellow believers. We can't truly love God while neglecting to love those who are created in His image. Through my experience with my ex-wife, I have learned that love is so vitally important in our daily lives—in our 'day-to-day' relationships, on the job, in the church, and among our family and friends. His love in and through us is so important that Jesus mentions its critical nature nine times in John 15:9-17. It is one of God's greatest concerns: that we learn how to love each other.

Walking Away

Shortly after our "convergence of forgiveness" toward each other, the Lord moved on my ex's heart, and she accepted Jesus as her savior. She left the "nation of Islam" religion and now serves the living God. She attends women's retreats on a monthly basis and studies the Bible diligently and daily. She has joined a church and is growing daily as she shares her faith with me and her children.

One day I asked her what had prompted her to receive the Lord as her savior. Her reply was, "I've been watching your life."

There were issues, hurts, and feelings that prevented the two of us from sharing the truth of God with each other over the intervening years. But my ex was wise enough to know that if we stayed our distance (disarming the bitterness and anger), we could still see the work of the

Lord in process. We cannot force a relationship of intimacy with someone, even if they would allow for the opportunity to share faith with us. However, we would be wise to understand that there are those who will watch us from a distance—and the brightness of His glory can shine sufficiently to cover that distance.

There is a lot of talk these days about following the example of Jesus by "accepting" and "affirming" people just as they are. The implication is that we must never confront them when they do something wrong. Yes, Jesus loved and accepted people, but He did *not* shrink back from confronting their sin, both in their hearts and actions. We are called and commanded to imitate Christ. We need to imitate His acceptance *and* His confrontation of the sin that separates us from Him and from each other. We need His help every day to show His love and His way to a world that daily spirals downward in the grip of the enemy. We, as believers, must show love just as Jesus did.

Are we in love with God, just as He is with us? If so, then we can do as He does. We can forgive and love one another by the power of His simple love working in and through us.

Thank you, Lord, for your love and forgiveness. Help us, by your Holy Spirit, to love others, as you have loved us. And, in so doing, help us to value, protect, and enrich the lives of those around us with your gift of love. Let us love one another.

ABOUT THE AUTHOR
Henry Washington – Simple Love

Written by Ted Hillberg

Henry is a "man among men," in every sense of the word. Henry is so consumed by the love of our Lord that he cannot help but walk into the very belly of hell to proclaim deliverance to the captives. As a professional mechanic, Henry builds cars. As a minister of the Most High, he builds men. As an ambassador of the kingdom, Henry unashamedly, and without fear or apology, invites all to enter into the consuming love of the Father. A recent example of Henry's exercise of his call to evangelism gives strong insight into who Henry is—and into the depth of his commitment to his simple, foundational love for his Savior. Recently Henry's job took him into the heart of the hellish territory of a white supremacist group. Now, Henry—who is African-American—stands at 6' 1"+ and weighs about 210 lbs. As such, he can be somewhat physically intimidating. It would have been very easy and "normal" for Henry to allow the natural antagonisms of the situation to control the circumstances. However, Henry—being totally consumed by the Love of God—intimately ministered to the leader of the group and interceded aggressively on behalf of a young girl who had been caught up in the web of hatred and bitterness. The result of his submission to the healing love of God was a strong witness to the delivering power of the King. Henry effectively planted seeds of forgiveness and love in the midst of a field of hate that the enemy was attempting to establish. The enemy had attempted to orchestrate the destruction of peoples' lives and hopes. But one man's submission to the plan of God resulted in the establishment of a monument testifying to the deliverance-power of God in the very center of the enemy's courtyard.

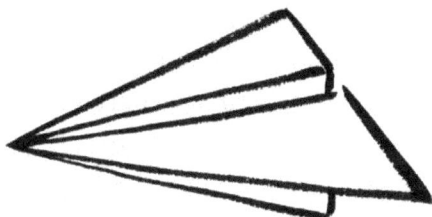

CHAPTER THREE

Simple Ministry

Buck Steele

When asked to write this chapter on simple ministry, I had in mind it would be an easy assignment. What could be so hard about simple? As it turns out, I've never experienced as much frustrating brain-strain trying to write anything—FVFR! Consequently, I felt like eradicating—pulling out by the roots—the word "simple" from the English language, at least in America. But despite the frustration from weeks of mental dredging, I finally dug up something that caused my belief in simple to reemerge. What I uncovered was some simple truths about the Man who personified simple. Since the One I'm referring to never changes, I knew this Man's simple approach to life had relevance for today, even in America—the land of the hi-tech, sprint-paced, low-maintenance lifestyle.

Simplicity, in my mind, is what made Jesus such an effective and accomplished person. Ironically, however, that same simple trait played a big part in getting Him hung by nails. The reason is that the religious rulers harbored a seething resentment for the simple but effective ways Jesus exposed their hypocrisy and dismantled their complex schemes of entrapment.

To embrace life as simply as Jesus did is quite remarkable. Here we have the man upon whose shoulders the greatest weight of responsibility has ever rested. Add to that the pressing weight of knowing He only had a few years to get the job done. And let's not forget the ever-present and foreboding weight He carried in knowing how it would all end. Yet from beneath the weight, Jesus still found time to be alone, pray, hang out with kids, attend weddings, and go to funerals. So where did He find the strength and stamina to be the main character in *The Greatest Story Ever Told*?

Getting Peace from God

A big part of the answer is found in a statement He made. Jesus said He never did anything unless He saw His Father do it. He applied the same simple rule to the things He said. In other words, Jesus had His mind on God. Because His mind was set on God, Jesus had perfect peace. Peace was a key element that enabled Jesus to be all He was, and to do all He did.

To illustrate the importance of having peace from God, let's imagine a day in Jesus' life when His peace was nothing more than an obscure thought. The morning begins in a glimmer of light but is soon overcast in a shadow of oppression. As the day wears on, the sky darkens and the weight of life looms heavier. Realizing His vision is starting to blur and His purpose is growing dim, the Son of Man peers up into heaven from whence His strength and stamina come.

But on this particular day when heaven's window opens, Jesus doesn't see His Father at peace and in control. Dad is out of control and in a frenzy. He's jerking chains, He's pulling levers, He's blowing whistles, He's barking orders, and He's slamming tranquilizers.

In utter dismay at the sight, Jesus just lowers His head and steps into a boat with His disciples. Within a few short hours a raging storm tears open the sea, threatening to destroy the boat and everyone onboard. Now do you suppose, after having witnessed His Father's frothing sweat frenzy, that Jesus is peacefully asleep in the bow of the boat? Not this time! He's freaking out with all the other frantic water-bailing disciples who have no peace. And why aren't they at peace? Well, it's probably because their minds are on themselves, the storm, and everything else but God.

The following morning Jesus and the boys, still shaking from last night's nerve-twisting ordeal, drift onto the opposite shore. No sooner do they step out of the boat than they're confronted by the snarling, screaming, wild man of the Gadarenes. Now, do you think that without the anchor of God's peace to secure Him, Jesus would stand His ground? Heck no! He would have been the lead inspiration for the disciples to perform their first miracle: running on the water!

Do you get the picture? Simply stated, life without peace can turn chaotic real quick.

Getting Understanding from God

By now you might be wondering what all this has to do with simple ministry. That's a good question with a good answer. First of all, simple ministry, simply defined, is the natural outflow of a simple life that's in vital union with God. The life-to-life connection to God is key.

To have this relationship requires we do one thing and not do another thing. One thing we need to do is *be transformed by the renewal of our minds*. We need to learn to think and act in a way God would if He were in our shoes. The thing we are not to do is *lean on our own understanding*. Our sub-standard logic and reason will collapse beneath the weight of God's will and purpose for

38

our lives. Don't get me wrong: logic, reason, and common sense all play an important, God-prescribed role in our lives. But all must come under the influence of God's Spirit.

The following story is a classic illustration of how God's Spirit transcends our reasoning abilities. Back in the 1930s a British aviator named Hanley Page drew up plans for a new airplane. When the plane finally emerged from the blueprints Hanley chose to be the first to fly the prototype. Once off the runway he pulled back on the controls, climbing higher and higher. At one point in his assent Hanley looked into the fuselage and saw a rat gnawing on some wires. Hanley knew if the rat chewed through the right wire the plane would go down. His first response was to turn back and land the plane as soon as possible. Common sense would tell you that. But before he could act on that thought, a thought of another origin entered his mind. This new thought was in direct opposition to his first and came more as an impulse: "Take the plane higher." Now if you were in the same situation, what would you do? I'm not sure what I would do. But I do know this, the urge to lean on my own understanding and forget the "God idea" would be strong. Hanley, however, in defiance to his will, reason, and emotions elected to obey the higher impulse. Climbing higher, Hanley ascended to a height where he saw the wisdom of God manifest. He was now flying at an altitude that wasn't conducive to the rat's life. Within moments the oxygen-starved rat dropped dead. All this occurred in less time than it would take for Hanley to follow the lead of his first thought. And who knows: had Hanley gone the course of his own understanding, would he had lived to tell about it?

Permit me now to deviate from talking about simple ministry to implementing it. I believe there are those of you who, having read this story, are aware of a few rats gnawing at the vital wiring of your life—rats of addiction or mental strongholds; rats gnawing on your relationships; or rats in your attitudes or circumstances. It seems like no matter what you do, the rats just keep gnawing. If this is the case, then I urge you to tune into God's frequency. You just might hear the Spirit's call to "fly higher." It may be that simple. Why not? Try it. Stretch out your wings. Dip into the thermal updraft of God's Spirit and let Him take you to the place where rats die and spirits live. Go the distance with Him, be sensitive to the wind and live.

Fly higher my beloved friend;
there is no limit to the height you may ascend.
Though the darkness surrounds you and the storms assail,
of this I can assure you, your faith in the Light will pierce the darkened veil.
So fly on my friend,
fly to your destiny wherein lies eternity, life beyond end.

The part that Spirit-governed thinking plays in a simple life and subsequent ministry should be clearer by now. But just to make sure we get this one, let's illustrate it. Let's imagine what a day in Jesus' life would look like if He chose to run the show from His own understanding.

The day begins much like any other—a good stretch and a yawn, reminiscence of last-night's dreams, then a quick mental scan of what needs to get done. The big one on today's list is to start putting the team together. So, with no time to waste, the Son rises with the sun. No sooner does He rise, however, than things go haywire. A dog chewed up one of His sandals, crows ate the morning meal, and the paperboy is either late, lost, or has wrecked his bicycle. To top it off, Starbucks is closed, and He's got one of those headaches coming on that only a stiff cup of java can cure.

Though totally dejected, the Son of Man pulls Himself together and does what He knows He's supposed to do. He peers up to heaven from whence His strength and stamina come. But like the time before when heaven's window opened, things are different. Instead of His usual "...My Beloved Son..." salutation, He overhears Pop bossing around the angels, cursing the incompetence of man and criticizing the Son for the rag-tag group of folks He hangs around with.

Picking up on the tension in the air, Jesus quietly slips away, closing heaven's window behind Him. Then in quite the same pose as Rodine's *The Thinker*, Jesus finds a nice rock to settle down on. "I've really got to think this one out," He mutters to a lizard doing pushups on a nearby rock. "You know," pointing to His reptilian friend, "not too long ago I honestly believed I could pick My team, at least half of them, by something as simple as prayerful, observant walks along the seashore. What was I thinking!? To pull this off, I need educated men, graduates from the University of Tarsus, men with degrees in business, communications, and linguistics. I need highly motivated men, the financially successful and politically savvy. I need men of vision, and throw in a good accountant. But only the best will do. All prospects will have to undergo thorough background checks, private eye investigations, genetic profiling, psychiatric evaluations, and lie-detector tests. "Oh, and I almost forgot," shaking His finger at the now bug-eyed lizard frozen between pushups, "when I've narrowed it down to twenty men, they'll all have to run the decathlon. The twelve highest scores get the job, maybe."

As ridiculous as this sounds, doesn't it sound a lot like men in their own understanding trying to do the simple things of God? Let's face it, if Jesus wasn't one with His Father, the gospels would read a lot differently. The fact is, they wouldn't be good news at all. They would just be a sad four-part commentary of a stressed-out visionary, who in His own feeble strength set out to accomplish the impossible. The saddest part of all would be the number of used, hurt, and bewildered people left in the wake of His reckless ruin.

The good news is that Jesus *was* one with His Father. Because the Two were one, Jesus could trust His Father's decision to have a known thief be the guardian of the purse. A carnal, un-renewed mind cannot and will not submit itself to these sorts of "unthinkable" ways of God. Because Jesus was mentally in tune with His Father, Jesus had the freedom to think beyond man's logical boundaries—so much so that He actually believed He could feed 5,000 men with a little boy's lunch.

Walking the same road in agreement with His Father produced an unshakable peace in Jesus' life. Because of that peace, He could easily turn aside from His own agenda to follow Spirit-led detours of compassion, like the one involving Jarius and his daughter. It's hard for a peace-less, driven man to be sensitive to surrounding needs, much less the silent cries for help.

In summary, the three main ingredients to a simple life and ministry are these:

1. A renewed mind dialed into God.

2. An abiding trust in God.

3. A stable peace.

All mixed together and baked in life's pressure cooker, this recipe will yield an anointing that will cause the "foolish" things of God to confound man's wisdom, and the "weak" things of God to bring down man's strongholds.

Taking the Kingdom by Violence

Because the ingredients of a simple life and ministry all sound so simple, what I'm about to say will sound contradictory. *It's not that simple.* We're in a war. If we are going to experience simple ministry, we are going to have to fight for it. Its' an ongoing battle to renew your mind in a world that bombards you day in and day out with thoughts and images that fly in the face of God. It's down-right difficult to stay simple in a world whose complex, bony fingers are constantly trying to prod and pry their way into your life.

To just sit back and trust God doesn't always work. At times our often passive forms of Christianity are going to have to display a little violence, like kicking over some money tables that stand in God's way or stomping some long bony fingers that have no business in our lives. It's kind of like peeling a banana. Most of the time that's a pretty simple operation. You just hold the thing in one hand and peel down the skin with the other. But every once in a while you get your hands on one of those rubbery-skinned things that, no matter how hard you try, you just can't pierce through the skin. So what do you do? You resort to violence! You stick the stupid thing in your mouth and bite the bitter stem off, or you take a knife to it! Yeah! I think you get the picture.

Attentiveness in a World of Distraction

Now let's hit home with this a little bit. Let's talk about a little techno-wonder-box otherwise known as a cell phone. Wow, what a great invention. That one electronic device has revolutionized the world. It's made life run a lot more smoothly and efficiently for a lot of people. ...But not for me! I'm still trying to figure out our 1986 microwave oven. Besides, even if I owned a cellphone, I don't think it would last more than a week under the barrage of paint, grease, weld spatter, and other abuses I'd put it through.

So if I don't own one, then why did I bring up the subject?

Let me explain it through a story. Imagine a day when the Son of Man packed a Samsung A570 on His hip. Jesus and the boys are kicking up dust through Samaria. At high noon they stop for a break at Jake's watering hole. Jesus wants to rest, but Pete and the gang are going into town to do some souvenir shopping. As they head out, Jesus reminds John to leave his cell phone on, just in case He needs to get in touch. With the boys gone, Jesus finds a place to kick back on the shady side of the well. Within minutes He's catching some much-needed "zzz's," when— you guessed it—the phone rings.

Jesus begrudgingly reaches for His phone and flips it open. John's gnarled face appears on the screen. "What is it John?" Jesus asks.

John answers, "Those guys started arguing again about who's gonna sit on your right and left side when your kingdom comes. I told 'em to knock it off or I was gonna call you. They wouldn't listen. So that's why I called. Sorry to bother you, but will you talk to 'em?"

Jesus just shakes His head and says, "You figure it out."

Wide awake now and sitting with His back against the warm stone wall of the well, Jesus scans the horizon. As He does, the image of a woman emerges out of the heat waves. She's alone and carrying a water jar on her shoulder. When she approaches the well, she sees the stranger and turns away. Sensing her timid spirit, Jesus greets her with a kind hello. Her only response is a quick glance and hesitant smile. She then turns to lower her jar into the well.

When it's drawn back up, Jesus asks her for a drink. She gestures for Him to drink. Jesus thanks her, drinks, and then begins to talk to her. She's not sure why, but within moments she feels relaxed and welcome in this stranger's presence. His acceptance of her invites her to open up in a way she's never opened up to anyone. The strangest part of all is this stranger seems to know her better than she knows herself.

Still not certain of what's going on, her parched spirit continues to drink from a well that's deeper than any she's ever drawn from before, and the water refreshes to a depth she's never known. With the windows of her soul open to His caring gaze, she asks Him, "Who are you?"

There's a contemplative pause. Then Jesus answers, "I am..."...and the phone rings to a blaring stanza of Stars and Stripes. Both are startled. Jesus grabs for the phone and tells the woman to hold her thought, then turns aside to answer the rude interruption. It's Pete. He's all excited about the great deal he got on a pair of genuine, *hecho en Mexico*, pig-skin sandals with real brass buckles.

"You want me to pick you up a pair," Pete asks, "to replace the one the dog chewed up?"

"Yeah," Jesus answers, "size ten. Just tell Judas to take it out of the road fund. And grab me a hot dog on your way back, put some sauerkraut and mustard on it, ditch the relish and onions. And you guys stay out of trouble. You don't want to see the inside of one of their jails. Oh, and on your way back, see if you can figure out that fig tree parable you stumbled over the other day. Okay, I gotta go, I have someone here I'm talking to."

"Who?" Pete replies.

"A woman, Samaritan woman."

"A what!?"

"Never mind, just head back before sundown." Click.

By this time the woman who, for the first time maybe in her life, felt valued and listened to, was now withdrawing behind the protection of her wall, feeling less important than the dust on her feet. When Jesus finally turns back to her and says, "Now where were we," she's already lifting her jar onto her shoulder.

"It was good talking to you," she says. "Maybe we'll see each other again sometime, but I have to go now," and she waves good-bye.

Although this story is fiction, the scenario plays out in real life every day. I'm sure you have been on the woman at the well's end of that deal a few times. I've been asked a number of times myself, "Would you mind if I put you on hold for a minute? I've got another call coming in." Well, if you really do want to know, I do mind. My time is valuable and I don't like spending it on elevator music. God forbid that we should miss something "important" because we chose to be attentive and respectful to the first person we were talking with. I believe if Solomon knew about cell phones, or any phone for that matter, he would have added another line to His infamous third chapter of Ecclesiastes: "there is a time to turn your phone on, and there is a time to turn it off."

Please hear me out on this. Here are some questions every one of us needs to consider seriously:

1. Am I being careful, respectful, and wise in the use of my technologies?

2. Are there any other bony fingers of intrusion robbing sensitivity and simplicity from my life?

48

3. Am I living the way God wants me to, or have I somehow been caught up in this hi-tech, sprint-paced, low-maintenance whirlwind called life?

Getting God on the Inside

In bringing this chapter one step closer to its end, I would like to share a true story with you that illustrates the power of Spirit-led simplicity. I was with a group of about 12-15 people in San Francisco. Our day began at a coffee house. While we were standing in line, I noticed an older woman come into the shop and survey the crowd. By the look on her face, I could tell she wasn't too happy with the thought of standing at the end of such a long line. Noticing that, I walked over and asked if she would like to take a place in line ahead of our group. She was delighted. So, I gave her my place, and I went back to the end of the line.

As it turns out, we ended up at the condiment table at the same time. I thought that was a little strange considering the number of people who were in line between us. But over the years I've learned to pay attention to those little oddities in life, many of which have turned out to be "God's finger" stirring up something good.

Sensing God's touch, I engaged in a light conversation with the woman. That led up to us going outside to sit at one of the outdoor tables. As it turns out, Carol was much like the woman at the well, not so much in lifestyle as much as in her thirst for different water. She was quite interested

49

in hearing about our outreach to the homeless people of her city. In turn, she related stories in her own life when she asked God for help and believed He gave it to her. Through more of her conversation, I realized the only relationship with God that Carol had ever known is what I refer to as a "God on the outside" relationship.

It was clear to me now why God orchestrated this coffeehouse encounter. He wanted to go from *God on the outside* to *God on the inside*. I told Carol about my observation. She was intrigued and wanted to know more. I shared a few more drinks of living water with her. Before we finished our coffee, she allowed me to pray with her. Then the phone rang—not really. Actually, she received the "Stranger at the well" into her heart. It was that simple.

To close the door on this chapter, I would like us to focus on something I've deliberately kept "secret" up to now. Early on, I wrote down the recipe for a simple life and its subsequent ministry. But in doing so, I left out the main ingredient, the binder that makes it all happen. The "secret" ingredient is *love*. Without love, this recipe doesn't bake. You may as well wad it up and cast it to the wind. Not only is love the catalyst, but it's the standard by which all else is measured. If my mind is genuinely being renewed, the evidence will show up in how I'm learning to love, accept, and forgive. If I'm just getting smarter, more creative, and more disciplined but not learning to love, then I'm deceived. I'm nothing more than a modern-day clanging cymbal, or to put it in more contemporary terms, I'm nothing more than loud, annoying static on the radio. Because Jesus loved, He kept His focus on God. Because His focus was on God, His focus was on love, for God is love. Out of love came trust, out of trust came peace, and out of it all emerged a Man whose simple life overcame the obstacles keeping us from knowing Him and His great love for us. By this love shall all men know we are His disciples.

ABOUT THE AUTHOR
Buck Steele – Simple Ministry

Written by Ted Hillberg

Buck is someone everybody should meet. He is a prophet who is uniquely gifted in his ability to make a clear proclamation of God's Word. As one of the most creative individuals I have ever met, Buck paints, writes, welds, speaks, and constructs. There is almost nothing Buck can't make in any medium, if it can just be envisioned. Buck is an ordained minister, and all those creative giftings unfold in their glory as he explains and teaches the words of our Lord. Buck is a man without any pretense, and under vastly different circumstances, he could be a well-renown teacher, writer, and speaker. However, Buck has chosen to impact a few people with the complete vastness of his giftings rather than "lightly touch" multitudes with watered-down impact. The simple devotion that drives his ministry to others comes through clearly in what he shares on the subject of simple ministry. I have enjoyed Buck's input into my and my family's life for nearly 40 years.

CHAPTER FOUR

Simple Faith

Andrew Mitchell

simple faith
simple vs. complicated
simple because of what it is...
a gift not something I work to get
no strings
free for the asking
simple because of who gives it to me
the Son of God
the Lamb of God
the Coming King

In order to understand the meaning of "simple faith," first we need to understand the meaning of "simple." Consider the following dictionary definitions of "simple" (borrowed from dictionary.com):

1. easy to understand, deal with, use, etc.: a simple matter; simple tools.

2. not elaborate or artificial; plain: a simple style.

3. not ornate or luxurious; unadorned: a simple gown.

Simple, right?

Simple is Not Easy

If, in the consultation of human reason, one would seek a misnomer, 'simple faith' would qualify. We don't think faith is simple. The misnomer part comes to mind because what we want to be possible through faith is usually impossible... for us. So, let's see: if I want something unreal to be real, I have to go to the most real place there is, stand on the edge of that, and pull up or down something from the other place. That sounds like anything but simple.

A lyric from a song by The Band has the line, "...simple and free, just you and me..." The simple and free part works if the "you" part is God. "Just" should be simple, right? The problem is that faith may involve more than God and me— more like me and... something or someone else. That's where we get messed up. We might have faith for God to save us, but our faith with respect to the rest of the world is usually another story.

Why is the world so difficult? I can have faith for God to do stuff in my life, and He does. But there's a line, sort-of, which I have a hard time crossing over in reality. I can't say just where that line is, but it involves *others—their* salvation, *their* sin, *their* health, wealth, and so on. Where and when does God get too small?

Nobody ever said faith was easy, but it is free. And again, maybe it's simple because it's one part of God's plan—like an ingredient in a recipe. Without it, the recipe won't work. Imagine baking a cake. Put salt instead of sugar in the recipe. Sugar is just part of the recipe, but without it, cake ain't cake. Faith and fear are like salt and sugar. And we get them mixed up. We have fear of what we could have faith for. Or we have fear of everything but God, and we have faith only in God as God. How about faith in God for solutions to every situation in life? Try that instead of fear. Try only fearing God and having faith in God for everything else, including Himself. I like that. Now, how?

Faith that Works

For me, "faith" means something like the word "just." Just God, just pray, just believe. Or it means the word "only." When I want to focus on something, I get other stuff out of the way. If you want to concentrate on something, you take steps to eliminate distractions.

I make stuff. When I use power tools to make stuff, I use every piece of protective gear I can—just so I can concentrate on what I am doing. If I forget my earmuffs, there's not only the immediate discomfort of my screaming saw but also the subtle stress of worrying about hearing loss as well. Those factors are both distractions that increase my risk and chance of failure. The same goes for every piece of protective gear I use. If I have them all in place, I'm as relaxed as I can be to accomplish my goal with the tool.

Now add all the other armor—righteousness, truth, salvation, gospel—and you begin to see how it works.

Now faith is the substance of things hoped for, the evidence of things not seen. (Hebrews 11:1, KJV)

Now without faith it is impossible to please God. (Hebrews 11:6a, ISV)

...the just shall live by his faith. (Habakkuk 2:4b, KJV)

Our faith is the victory that overcomes the world. (1 John 5:4b, ISV)

Simple faith is faith that works. Faith without fact or reality is dead. Substance means *real*, no matter what air you breathe.

Faith for Fixing?

When I first began to believe in God and care about Him, He gave me a simple test. Could I believe Him to be a God who cared about the little, nagging, drive-me-crazy parts of my life? I used to lose my car keys on a regular basis... like just before I needed to leave to be on time to work. If I were God at that point and saw this pathetic dilemma, I would have chuckled and turned one of Andrew's fingers into a car key. "There ya go, son, problem solved."

It's obvious why we can't be our own god: we just want to solve problems and move on to the next dilemma. "Can we fix it? ...Yes we can." God isn't like that because He has no sin in Him. That's why we always want to fix things... something down deep is really wrong. We know all about "fix" because we know all about "broke." God wants to have a relationship with us where we know better than we know anything else that we need Him. His goal is not to "fix it," but to transform us into a new being, day-by-day. When we see the reality (glory) of His idea for solution, direction, and goal, we are not only relieved, but delighted, astounded, and stoked. "I once was lost but now am found, 'twas blind but now I see," as the lyric goes. Once God has shown me where my car keys are, then I can go somewhere.

Now the question is, where do I go? If I go off on my own, back to my own frantic little agenda and offer a brief "thank you Jesus" over my shoulder like, I-can-handle-it-now-thank-you, then I've wasted God's grace. I need to look to Him for what is next.

I remember as a boy there was one uncle who used to delight us kids with one amazement or another. After he had performed one of his jokes or tricks, we'd just hang around and wait for him to do something else, like take us out for "black cows" (root beer floats) or stand on his head and play a kazoo. Typical kids we are with God, and we need to hang around for His next act, even if we don't get the point of His dazzling us in the first place. We think He is entertaining us with little jolts of his almightiness, but He knows us, and He knows what we really need. He wants to win us over to a lifetime of heart-to-heart, one-on-one. There is much that concerns and delights Him, and He wants to share it all with us. If we get together really and truly, it's because of Him. That's why whenever we get together, He shows up. Simple... and the only time unnecessary hassles come are when we get together for any other reason besides Him.

We alone, on our own, are the goal of heaven's enemies. We in Christ are so much more than victory. It will take eternity to see.

The True Purpose of Faith

So, what does God want from us?

A woman from Samaria came to draw water. Jesus said to her, "Give me a drink."

John 4:7 (ESV)

Could you imagine Jesus Christ being weary and thirsty for you to put your faith in Him instead of trusting in your life experience? I have faith that has been given to me. It is my decision how to use it. It is like the one cake of bread the disciples had with them on the boat with Jesus after He had fed the thousands. "What...? We have no bread?"

Now they had forgotten to bring bread, and they had only one loaf with them in the boat. And [H]e cautioned them, saying, "Watch out; beware of the leaven of the Pharisees and the leaven of Herod." And they began discussing with one another the fact that they had no bread. And Jesus, aware of this, said to them, "Why are you discussing the fact that you have no bread? Do you not yet perceive or understand? Are your hearts hardened? Having eyes do you not see, and having ears do you not hear? And do you not remember? When I broke the five loaves for the five thousand, how many baskets full of broken pieces did you take up?" They said to [H]im, "Twelve." "And the seven for the four thousand, how many baskets full of broken pieces

59

did you take up?" And they said to [H]im, "Seven." And [H]e said to them, "Do you not yet understand?"

Mark 8:14-21 (ESV)

In my hands, the faith I have looks like nothing, even though I've seen Jesus do incredible things for others with their faith. When situations challenge me, that faith in my hands will fail. But if I put that faith in the hands of Jesus Christ, He will change everything—me, my faith, the situation, and others. In His hands, the little lump of my clutching will be broken and blessed beyond my vision or expectation. It will then be immeasurably adequate to meet needs of every situation. Keeping our faith to ourselves and what we know amounts to nothing. Putting our faith in Christ produces abundant life. What do you want? Nothingness or abundant life? When we give Him our faith (e.g. our water), He gives *Himself* to us.

Jesus answered her, "If you knew the gift of God, and who it is that is saying to you, 'Give me a drink,' you would have asked [H]im, and [H]e would have given you living water."

John 4:10 (ESV)

For the Lamb which is in the midst of the throne shall feed them and shall lead them unto living fountains of waters: and God shall wipe away all tears from their eyes.

Revelation 7:17 (KJV)

God wants to give us something we've only had the promise of and not the fact of. Jesus Christ is that gift—His death and resurrection, His Word, His Holy Spirit, and He Himself—our coming King. The cyclic and chronic failures in our lives (our "broken wells") are due to our sin heritage. Jesus Christ is the future of our lives the minute we quit believing our past and start believing in Him.

Whoever believes in me, as the Scripture has said, 'Out of his heart will flow rivers of living water.'

John 7:38 (ESV)

We are in the thick of God's wonderful war here, and we are seeing the significance of every individual in God's plan for victory.

God gave me a sign on Good Friday last week. I was in a lonely outdoor job-space. I was doing my work there—getting some materials out of a shed. In front of the shed is a concrete slab with dirt and weeds all around. As I was closing the door of the shed, God spoke. God told me to ask Him for a sign, but I sort-of doubted His voice. So, He *commanded* me to ask Him for a sign. I got the picture and asked. Immediately where I stood, He said, "Turn around and look down on the ground." I doubted again, but remembering the rebuke in God's command, I repented and obeyed. When I turned around and looked down, my eyes fell on blood stains smeared on the concrete slab. This was actual creature blood—God only knows what type of creature. I was immediately stymied and baffled. My mind did not try to understand. I simply asked God to reveal the meaning in His time.

That night as we gathered to pray in the Hillberg home for our once-a-month time, God began to speak. Jesus told us that His atonement was absolutely for *whoever*, *wherever* we set our feet. And his atonement is for whoever stands with us. This means His atonement is for all of us, as we continue to walk together because of Him. He is who He is in our lives because of *His will* and *our confession* of who He is. The authority of His will flows from who He is and who we believe He is. Even the powers of hell know who we are because Christ has called our names as blessed. Christ calls us blessed in response to the will of our Father in heaven, as we confess Jesus as the Christ, the Son of the living God.

Let this be our response to any and all unbelief in our lives and in the lives of those God calls us to. We are to move in unison and set our will toward the redemption of Christ each day and all day.

It's that simple.

ABOUT THE AUTHOR

Andrew Mitchell – Simple Faith

Written by Ted Hillberg

Andrew is one unique man of God. Andrew is the guy, who, when you ask, "How is it going?," he actually tells you. He is one of the few people who can answer the question, "What time is it?" with four paragraphs of riveting, descriptive revelation. When you meet him on the street, you best set aside 20-30 minutes, for Andrew will not let you go until he has encouraged your walk in faith. Andrew's heritage includes four to five generations of pastors and missionaries. Andrew himself was born in a foreign land on the mission field. Through this heritage, and through his consuming appetite to see God's plan of redemption established everywhere, Andrew sees things that go unnoticed by the average man. I can't explain in words the level of complete dependence, obedience, and faith in God that

Andrew operates in. All I know is that his insight and ministry results in an increase in the ability to see, hear, and know God. Andrew can take the most confusing and confounding situation and, in faith, remove the layers of confusion to reveal the sovereign working of God. To me, and others who have personal relationships with him, Andrew personifies the saint who has been gifted with the gift of faith for the edification and encouragement (building up) of the Body, (cf. 1 Cor. 12, 1 Cor. 14, Eph. 4).

CHAPTER FIVE

Simple Expression

Ted Hillberg

Simple Expression Defined

A kiss is the simplest expression of your love. To kiss your lover is an undeniable, unchallenged demonstration, publicly testifying of your commitment of love to a specific object of that commitment. Curiously, it was that same, simple act that Judas used to identify the target of his broken commitment. It was the one act that would have been "un-thinkable"—an act of betrayal.

Society today markets the need to expand on this simple expression of love. A kiss is no longer sufficient in expressing our love and devotion. For some reason, we need a more complex expression: we need to buy a diamond, book a cruise, plan an extravagant celebration, etc., etc. However, these additional gestures are never enough. At every anniversary or subsequent expression, we need to "go to the next level," take another step up in the intensity or quality of the expression. Simple is no longer enough. Simple has come to be defined as "simplistic," or as something of "lesser value" than a more complex rendition.

I grew up in a church denomination that was enraptured with the complex interpretations of how to live, how to worship, what was going to happen next, and who was going to heaven in first place. Over years of reading the words of God in the Scriptures, one thing has become very clear to me: the "people of God" get into the most difficulty when they make the simple commands of the Lord into something complex.

God got so frustrated at the convoluted rules and complexities the Israelites made up. The people of Israel continually instituted complex rules in addition to God's direct instructions. For this reason, in Micah 6:8, God finally—and plainly—boiled down what He wanted most into these simple instructions:

Here's what I want you to do: deal with others in a just and fair manner, extend as much mercy to others as you would have them extend to you, and finally, stop acting like you're so important. Instead, walk through life in a humble manner, always with God at your side.

Micah 6:8 (Ted's paraphrase)

This is my favorite verse in the whole Bible. I have attempted to make this verse the foundation of how I live, also instructing my sons in its foundational value. I have found the Epistle of James to be the most practical guide for "walking out" these foundational principles in daily interactions. Simply put, if you want to see if I believe and live out the precepts of Christ, then look at how I extend mercy to those who injure me. See whether I transact with others in a way that assures them that I have been more than fair and just. See whether what you see is what you get. See whether I act as if I am more important than others, or whether I consider others of equal importance to myself. See if I am living what I am preaching. If I am doing these things, then I am living out these verses.

In Matthew 5, Jesus gives us the "Sermon on the Mount." Read the first 12 verses (the Beatitudes). You will see constant descriptions and examples of what we could easily describe as the "simple things" of life on earth.

Without any doubt, we all want to be blessed by God. With that being the case, we should heed Jesus' advice and live like this:

- be intimately acquainted with, and constantly aware of our total need for Him (poor in spirit, v. 3).

- be truthful in the expression of our grief (mourn, v. 4).

- be aware of our position in Him, and our residency in His kingdom (humble, v. 5).

- be "driven" in our hunger to know, and be changed by His Grace (hunger & thirst, v. 6).

- be forgiving, full of understanding and grace (merciful, v. 7).

- be pure in our thoughts, desires, and intentions (pure, v. 8).

- be peacemakers, slow to anger, quick to reconcile (peacemakers, v. 9).

- be willing to suffer wrong to see right prevail (persecuted for righteousness, v. 10).

- be more focused on His will and purpose, than our comfort and station in life (v. 11, 12).

Looking at this "list," we can see it is really an expansion of Micah 6:8. We see that the call to "deal justly" is reflected in the admonitions of verses 9-11. The principle of "extending mercy" can be seen in verses 7 and 9. And the injunction to walk "humbly with our God" is easily seen in the examples given in verses 3-6 and 8. These are simple directions on how to live a simply rewarding life, God's way.

Simple Expression at Work in...

At the risk of giving a "formula" or "hidden secrets," below I set forth some guidelines for how I try to express the grace of God in my relationships. I give descriptions and explanations to help you understand my thinking. I've grouped these guidelines according to the type of relationship addressed.

Before I give the list, I will include the Scripture references that underwrite these principles of "simple expression." Look these Scriptures up for yourselves; many references apply to more than one principle.

Genesis 18:19;
Proverbs 3:3-4, 4:25-27, 10:9, 12:19-22;
Matthew 5:3,7,43-48, 6:12,6:14-15, 11:29,
*   20:26-27, 23:12;*
Exodus 18:21, 15:33, 16:13, 22:4, 24:17,19;
Luke 6:31, 14:10-11, 16:10, 17:3-4, 22:24-27;
Deuteronomy 9:4-29, 16:19-20;
Ezekiel 18:7-9;
John 8:31-32;
Ephesians 4:2, 5:21;
James 4:10;
2 Samuel 22:21;

Micah 6:8;
Romans 12:3,10;
Philemon 2:3-11, 4:8;
1 Peter 2:12, 3:9, 5:5-6;
Job 5:11, 27:4-6, 29:14;
1 Corinthians 13:4;
Colossians 3:12-13;
Psalm 15, 24:3-5, 25:9, 40:10, 51:6, 89:14, 147:6;
Galatians 6:14;
Titus 1:7-8.

Family

LIGHT/HUMOR - not everything is life or death; remember, none of us gets out of this alive.

HUMILITY - someday, you will be a peer with your son or daughter; eventually they will grow up to be your brother or sister.

DISCERNMENT - pick the important battles to fight; sometimes just say "yes" because you've already used too many "no's".

GRACE - what you "bind" and "loose" on earth will be bound/loosed in heaven; give the same grace you hope to receive.

Friends

LISTEN - you can't listen with your mouth open.

HONOR - when a friend asks for your help, give it without strings; and, if possible, without your sage advice.

LOYALTY / STEADFASTNESS - everything is or can be covered completely by the blood of Christ.

Customers

DOUBLE HONOR - always give more than what is expected.

EXCELLENCE - perform your duties knowing that your real customer is your Father in Heaven.

RESPECT - the customer is not always right, but the servant doesn't have a voice.

Co-workers / Employees

ESTEEM - regardless of our vocational position, we are all equally loved, children of God; give respect to all.

MINISTER - our prime purpose in all transactional relationships is always to minister God's grace and Love.

HELP - treat every request by your co-workers as if they were your "customers."

ENCOURAGE - most people feel—rightfully or not—that the odds are stacked against them; sometimes, the most valuable thing you can do is encourage someone to combat the temptation to give up or give in to the inevitable failure or disappointment.

Creditors

TRUTH – as hard as it may be, resist the temptation to create a "plausible excuse"; God says that the truth shall set you free.

INTEGRITY - this is the foundational character reputation, which will give place to credible ministry.

PRIORITY - the rightful priority of debt repayment supplants the right to satisfy wants or desires; "owe no man anything, except the debt of love."

Debtors

MERCY – "The measure by which you measure, shall be used to measure you"; beware.

HEALING – "Whatever you bind on earth, shall be bound in Heaven; whatever you loose on earth, shall be loosed in Heaven."

FORGIVENESS – "Father, forgive us our debts; [just] as we forgive our debtors."

Acquaintances

REDEEM - mankind has been ravaged by the destroyer; assume that every acquaintance has been devalued by the enemy, and treat each appointment as an opportunity to provide redemption (of time, self-worth, affirmation, love, hope, etc.), not an opportunity for you to exact additional payment.

PROCLAIM - a day of "acceptance" of the Lord; don't preach, but truthfully proclaim His wonders and grace.

RESTORE - the only effect we may be able to have on acquaintances is the restoration of "open lines of communication" with the Father; this restoration can be accomplished without verbal interaction—just your intercession at the throne.

Beggars

GIVE - stop trying to 'out-guess' God; most people beg (ask) because they do not have something they need or desire.

WISE - pay attention to the obvious: give to affect the need, not the greed.

TEACH - the prime lesson from the opportunities to give is to teach us about giving; we are able to give because we have been blessed with surplus.

Verses and Thoughts

In this section, I want to look deeper at some familiar verses from Scripture. I'll explain how each verse has helped to form and verify my understanding of how to express my love for my Savior in simple and solid interaction and communication.

Let your yea be yea and your nay be nay. (cf. Matthew 5:37)

Most of the time, I have heard this verse used in connection with a teaching on "do not curse," or something to that effect. However, if you look at the context of the whole passage, I believe a case can be made for the interpretation that the point of this directive is to simply "say what you mean, and mean what you say."

One of my hot button topics with my boys has been that "a man is nothing if he does not have integrity of his word." If you say a thing, mean it. If you make a commitment, follow through, regardless of the immediate cost. The long-term cost of not being a "man of your word" far exceeds whatever the short-term cost (or inconvenience) of honoring that vow.

I say "vow" because that is what it is: your word is your "vow." Your word does not need to be enhanced or qualified by an oath. If you say "yes" or "no," that is enough: back it up, always. This reduces all interaction and communication to a very simple plane. No more is it a matter of "how strongly did you mean it?" or, "I didn't really mean what I said." From a "man's point of view," your word (and the integrity of it) does not become cluttered up with the emotions of the moment. If you say it, it becomes fact— cast in stone, as it were.

I love the Nike commercial, where they say, "Just do it!" One of my friends said that the phrase—"Just do it!"—could sum up my contribution to this book. In a lot of ways, he was correct; but, there is more to what God wants me to share than just that simple phrase alone.

Behold, the tongue! (cf. James 3:5)

These verses go hand-in-hand with the above. There is extreme power in your words (tongue)—not only in what you say, but also in what the hearer *believes* you said. If you truly consider your word your vow, then you will see yourself obliged to honor not only what is expressed, but also what the receiver believes is your intent. Truly, the "sin of omission" is just as great as the "sin of commission." When you communicate in such a way as to lead the hearer to an untrue understanding, there is no difference between that and a lie.

In addition, when you have adopted the conviction that your word is your bond, and when you have gotten tired of (repeatedly) having to pay for implied commitments that you had no intention of expressly making, at that point, you will become more careful and selective regarding what you allow to come out of your mouth. Once again, the captain gains control of the rudder of the ship, and thereby, the course of travel.

Except you become as a little child... (cf. Matthew 18:3)

God calls us to "child-like" faith and trust in His provision for life. The world would describe this as "childish," but don't believe it. The fact is, God calls us to a pure, simple, completely dependent relationship with Him, well exemplified by the father-child dynamic. "Childish," by definition, is impure, selfish, and immature. The "child-like" relationship of trust in the Father, by contrast, is characterized by the following attributes: pure, un-jaded trust in His righteous decisions, total dependence upon His total power to supply all needs, and the mature realization that He is Lord of all and that His words are the ultimate authority. That is a complete description of unselfish, total maturity.

A. W. Tozer wrote a book regarding the importance of an accurate understanding of the attributes of God. Complex theological studies have expanded human understanding of the attributes of God into something akin to a ten-thousand-word thesis to be dissected by Ph.D.'s for decades as they consider the conjugations of verbs and the declensions of nouns used to depict the various (human) descriptions of the essence of God's character. Those attributes are commonly enumerated as follows: omnipotence, omniscience, immutability, omnipresence, holiness, and eternality. These are the six primary attributes ascribed to God.

When you look at these attributes in regards to their "simple" definitions, they become these: all-powerful, all-knowing, unchangeable, everywhere-present, always good, and ever-living (without beginning or end). The "child's rendition" of these attributes is this: "My God (Father) is bigger and stronger than all others"; "My God (Father) sees everything and knows everything"; "My God (Father) is everywhere"; and "My God (Father) never makes a mistake and will always love me and show that love in how he treats me."

Tozer states that our understanding and practice of our faith will only rise to, and not exceed, the quality of our knowledge of the greatness of the object of our faith. When we are fully convinced that our God is King of Kings, Lord of All, the Alpha and Omega, Holy and Righteous in all His ways, Redeemer, Savior, Healer, and Rewarder of those who diligently seek Him, then—and only then—will our practice and expression of faith rise to the level of "a holy and acceptable sacrifice of worship" to Him. A correct vision of our God will result in an accurate interpretation of how we are to reflect His character in our expressions and interactions with those with whom we are appointed to have relationship.

Summary

Man was created in the very image of God. In the Garden, God was on His throne, and mankind walked in perfect submission and right relationship to that Authority. Driven and consumed by an all-encompassing love for the Creator-Father, man's words, thoughts, and actions were the natural response and out-growth of that perfectly aligned relationship. However, just like Lucifer, man became dissatisfied with the boundaries of God's love, and he decided that he should "exalt his own throne" and become like the Most High. At that point, man "stole" the Creator's rightful place to be on the throne of man's life. Man set his own "Self" upon it as the ruler.

To this day, we still wrestle with ownership of that throne and over who or what will set our course, move our hearts, motivate our actions, guide our relationships, and direct our paths. Even as believers, we still have a tendency to enthrone Self on the throne of our lives. It is so subtle that we are scarcely aware of it happening. Because we are born rebellious, we have a hard time recognizing our rebellion. The promotion of our ways (self-determination, self-reliance, self-sufficiency, self-esteem) seems perfectly normal. There may be many times that we are willing to share the "throne," and even to sacrifice our ego or rights. But, it is nearly impossible to willingly "de-throne" ourselves. We imagine that no one besides ourselves has the right to control our lives—not even God.

When we become believers, we re-establish the right relationship with God. We, who are created, worship God through our living. This cannot be done if the throne of our lives is occupied by Self. Either God is the "I Am"; or we are the "I Am" of our lives. This is why even the "good works" of our lives are as "filthy rags," as they are done from an authority of Self. Only when the stolen throne has been rightly returned to God—for His occupation and the establishment of His authority—will our works become an "acceptable sacrifice of worship." The Lord Himself stated this truth when he said, "If any man come after me, let him deny himself, take up his cross, and follow me." Peter reiterates this truth in his life—and calls us to the same vow—in 1 Peter 1:9, saying, "I am crucified with Christ, nevertheless I live; yet not I, but Christ liveth in me."

"Denying Thyself" (as in Matt 16:24) is not the same as self-denial. I don't believe any of the real martyrs of the faith saw themselves as martyrs. The fact is they never *saw themselves* at all. That is the point. Paul said, "For me to live is Christ," and "it is not I (Paul) who lives, but Christ living in me."

Fulfillment in Christ means fulfilled *by* Christ. We need to return to the original relationship of being consumed by and for the very presence of God—in all aspects of our lives. It has to become intimate—the burning fire at our very core. Our God is an "all consuming" God; and to be one with Him requires an "all consuming" commitment rooted in an unfiltered covenant of love. It is ultimately *His love* to us, for us, and in us—and it's all for Him.

In summary, simply put: God is great! He is King of all, and He is all-powerful! He is the very essence of love perfected! All He does is pure and righteous. He is the "Ultimate Father," wholly committed to the protection, provision, care, and training of His beloved sons and daughters.

If you indeed believe that, then act like it! The discipline of living in that way is called *maturity*. This may sound too simple. But it is the sum total of faith and faith-driven actions. Search the Bible for an accurate and complete understanding of the knowledge of God. Then let that knowledge be your "standard" of life.

God is Love. He is moved to act on our behalf by the pure—holy and righteous—expression of that love in justice and mercy. He alone is God, and we are His people—joint heirs with the Son to receive all the gifts He is anxious to give. All He requires is that we submit our will to live a true reflection of His love to and for others, in all we say and do. He simply calls us to do this: *Do justly, love mercy, and walk humbly with our God.*

Kiss the Son, lest you die.

ABOUT THE AUTHOR
Ted Hillberg – Simple Expression

Written by Ted Hillberg

What I have learned from and through the men listed above has formed how I live my life today. While I may not have the gifts of knowledge and wisdom to the extent that these others have, I do have a practical understanding and experience of how those gifts have worked themselves out in the way I perform my job and interact with those whom God puts in my path. What I put forth in my chapter is not "5 Principles to a Killer Christian Life," but rather, I submit some strong principles that God has "burned into my soul." In turn, I would have these burned into the hearts of my sons also. I have had the opportunity—over the years of business dealings—to pass some of these same godly principles of living on to some of the men, women, boys, and girls with whom I have enjoyed God-orchestrated relationships over the years. As Mordecai said to Esther, "Who knows whether you were appointed for such a time as this?" (Esther 4:14). Every relationship and interaction we have is an opportunity for someone to see the unique gift that God has created us to be. And it is an opportunity to reflect precisely those attributes of His glory that people need to see and experience at that very moment of interaction. These are living relationships, and His will cannot be accomplished for them without our having a living, vital relationship with Him—a relationship that is "new every day with His mercies." I pray that as we all share what God has taught us, you will reaffirm your commitment to know, experience, and express the "simple" response and testimony of your love for Him. Keep it simple, Saint, and the wounded and wandering of the world will beat a path to the foot of the cross.

TRIBUTE TO TED

"A man who has friends must himself be friendly, but there is a friend who sticks closer than a brother."

Cf. Proverbs 18:24

When I think of Ted Hillberg, this verse readily comes to mind! I have known him for a little over thirty years, during which our two families became very close as we raised our children together and spent a lot of time in each other's homes doing life together. I can honestly say that Ted became one of the closest friends of my life. We were both passionate about worship and the Kingdom of God as we sought to follow Jesus in our respective journey through life. Ted was the kind of guy who had your back in every way you could imagine. He served actively and faithfully on the board of my itinerant ministry, New World Music Ministries, for about ten years. Our families would go on vacations and see movies together, and we laughed a lot!

In my opinion, Ted Hillberg is one of the finest examples of a friend I can think of, and I count it an honor to have been asked to contribute a chapter to this book that is reflective of his passion for worship and the Kingdom of God!

Caleb Quaye

I am writing this in remembrance of my loving friend and brother, Ted "Hillbery." He possessed an insight along with the ability to accurately understand who a person was. These qualities gave him the upper hand to insult you, with his loving smile, which then would get you to join in the laughter about yourself. What stood out the most to me was discovering how much love was in Ted.

God used Ted, as well as Caleb Quaye, to help mold my life into a man with a heart that knows how to love. When Ted approached me and asked me to write a chapter about "Love," I thought he was teasing me, but he was for real. I will always cherish in my heart Teddy's great insight of people.

One of my fondest memories of Ted was at the Caleb's home. My son Sultan was a baby at the time, sitting by my knee, crying, and wanting to be picked up and loved. I was not responding to him, and Ted was standing behind me, with folded arms. He gave me one of his looks. I knew he meant business, so I picked up my son into my arms. That moment changed me. I would come to find out later in our friendship that Ted was someone who had looked for that kind of love from his own father as a child. So, thank you Ted for touching my heart to love my son and daughter. We know Ted is in his loving Father's arms right now. Heavenly Father, I thank you that you placed Ted in my life to complete the healing process in my heart to possess a Heart of Love. I will always love the Hillberg family. Thank you, Ted, in the name of Jesus Christ, Amen.

Henry Washington

I first met Ted in the early eighties. At the time we were both holding tight to the life line of salvation while trying to swim in a religious sea of ideas, programs, and errant teaching. Although saved, we were still lost. Ted smoked cigarettes, which conjured up a few religious spirits— driving a wedge between him and the more sanctified saints. I was one of those who judged him secretly but soon realized his external "sin" wasn't who he was. Ted was real and really did care about what people thought, but not to the extent that he would masquerade behind a "I hope you approve of me if I do this or don't do that" mask. Ted's love for his family, church, and the lost helped me realize most words are better understood by demonstration with less talk, even if you did have a cigarette hanging out the side of your mouth :) I am a better man because a better man taught me a few things about what it means to love, serve, and befriend with hands, feet, and an old Cadillac that would accept the challenge of any deer that dared jump in front of it. Thanks Ted, looking forward to eternity with you.

Buck Steele

Ted is a treasure I discovered years ago, buried in a field of generational dreams broken by industrialism, revolution, and world war. I felt safe around Ted because of his honesty and courage. He was not ashamed of the wounds life had dealt him, and over time, those wounds became like the scars of our Lord's cross.

Ted reminds me of the Holy Grail in the Indiana Jones movie. And, yes... I did find him in the "church" as we knew it at the time. I felt secretly honored and wealthy to have discovered this treasure. Simply hidden amongst all the bejeweled and effort-encrusted relics of human endeavor, to seem godly, spiritual, upright and appropriate, Ted brought me the blood of Christ and helped secure the worldly reality of my salvation. He neither hid nor paraded his wounds, but my discovery of them led me more to Jesus. Ted was not about performance. He was about relationship with God—ask anyone who really knew him. He was the friend to me that I never knew I needed. I'd been searching for a heart of gold for myself, but I found it in someone else—and he shared it with me. So, in case you were wondering where to find the greatest treasure of life, look no further. "Others" is where you will find it.

Andrew Mitchell